BAD LUCK OR BAD BUSINESS?

*13 Most Common Tax Mistakes
Made by Business Owners*

WILLIAM G. CUMMINGS, CPA

DISCLAIMER

This publication is designed to provide information in regard to the subject matter covered. It is sold with the understanding that William G. Cummings and the publisher are not engaged in rendering legal, accounting, or other professional advice. If the reader needs such advice, he or she should seek the services directly with a competent professional.

The purpose of this book is to educate. The author and any affiliated companies shall have no liability or personal responsibility to any person or entity with respect to any loss or damage caused, or alleged to be caused, directly or indirectly, by the information in this book.

To illustrate his points, the author makes liberal use of actual cases. Unless otherwise stated, all of the cases describe fictional characters and situations. Any resemblance to persons, living or dead, is purely coincidental.

Copyright © 2013 William G. Cummings, CPA
All rights reserved.
ISBN: 1492275905
ISBN 13: 9781492275909
Library of Congress Control Number: 2013915988
CreateSpace Independent Publishing Platform, North Charleston, SC

For more information you can to write me or visit my website:
1304 South De Soto Ave., Suite 303
Tampa, FL 33606
813-374-9676
bcummings@tfamail.com
Williamcummingscfo.com

Acknowledgments

I would like to thank my wife, Kimberli, with whom I share a wonderful life and who helps me enjoy every minute of every day. To my wonderful children, Shadia, Tarek, Kristina, Heather, and Holly, for always accepting me, unconditionally, and helping me have fun in life. I would also like to thank my mentors, Tom Moriarty, Eric Jacobsen, Dan Franz, and Jerry Angel, for encouraging me to go into business for myself. To my coaches, Ed and Dominique, who encouraged me to write this book, thanks!

TABLE OF CONTENTS

PROLOGUE:
OVERTAXED?

"The hardest thing in the world to understand
is the income tax."

ALBERT EINSTEIN

ONE of the smartest men of the last century, a particle physicist, said that the income tax code is the hardest thing in the world to understand. That should give you an idea of the challenge that lies ahead for most individuals and businesses as they file their taxes this year. Furthermore, most people are unhappy with the amount of taxes they pay. They are unhappy with the IRS and the current volume of tax code that is very difficult to understand. As a certified public accountant (CPA), I understand your pain. I have spent over twenty-five years in the industry trying to help my clients pay the least amount in taxes.

In fact, prior to my current role as president of Cummings Financial Organization, I worked as a chief financial officer (CFO) for a financial services company for fifteen years. I had many roles: cash flow management, reducing taxes, risk management, succession planning, budgeting, etc. All the normal stuff a CFO would do.

I found that as a CFO, I spent a lot of time planning and trying to pay the least amount of taxes for the company. Often, the company paid fewer taxes than I, its CFO, did, and the company had significantly more income than I did!

This was a big "aha" moment for me, as it occurred to me that some of the most successful "big" companies paid fewer taxes than I did. I knew that the key to paying the least amount of taxes was done through proactive tax planning. So why doesn't this translate to most businesses? Well, I blame the accountants.

The traditional accounting model is broken. Traditional accountants each do hundreds of returns. They are so busy preparing returns that they do not have time to do proactive tax planning. That is one of the reasons I decided to start my own firm. I knew that people needed my expertise in helping them reduce their taxes.

So is there a "silver bullet" to reducing your tax bill? Yes, there is, and it is called proactive tax planning. That means reviewing your taxes before year's end to make sure you are using every legal deduction and loophole possible. Remember, tax preparation is not the same as tax planning. The former is recording history and the latter is making history. Tax planning is being creative within the rules outlined by the IRS code. My wife is an artist, and I like to tell her that I am creative as well—just with taxes.

I often come across people who ask me what I do for a living. If I tell them I am a CPA, the typical response is, "I already have a CPA" or "You must be busy in April." I finally changed my response to what I do for a living. I now say, "I am a CPA who specializes in helping my clients legally pay the least amount of taxes." I still have a few people who will respond, "Well isn't that what all CPAs do?"

There lies the other problem—the public thinks that if they pay their CPA or do their taxes on their own, they are paying the least amount in taxes. That is a bad assumption in that, as stated previously, you are just recording history and not proactively doing tax planning. Remember, the tax code changes every year, so that alone should be just cause for you to do proactive tax planning.

PROLOGUE: OVERTAXED?

If you're a business owner like me, the health and success of your business determines what kind of life you live, the kind of retirement you achieve, and the security you create for your family. Taxes are one of your biggest expenses, so why wouldn't you spend a considerable amount of time trying to reduce your taxes and put that money in your pocket as opposed to giving it to the IRS?

Many people out there just don't know that tax planning is the key to reducing their tax bill. I often tell people, "What you don't know can hurt you." That is one of the reasons I am writing this book. I want to make you aware of the biggest mistakes that the majority of people make.

By no means is this book meant to be a "how-to" book or a self-help book with detailed tax code and strategies for your personal situation. That book would be so voluminous that nobody would read it. The tax strategies I come up with for my clients come from years of schooling, passing a CPA exam, twenty-five years of accounting experience, and becoming a certified tax coach. My clients are not "do it yourselfers," and they pay me for the tax savings I provide them. That is the true value of tax planning: tax savings.

As you review this book for the most common tax mistakes that businesses make, consider if you have made these mistakes. Better yet, when was the last time your accountant presented you with creative tax-saving ideas?

CHAPTER 1

MISTAKE #1:
FAILING TO PLAN

"There is nothing wrong with a strategy to avoid the payment of taxes. The Internal Revenue Code doesn't prevent that."

WILLIAM H. REHNQUIST

THE first mistake is the biggest mistake of all. It's failing to plan.

I don't care how good you and your tax preparer are with a stack of receipts on April 15. If you didn't know you could write off your kid's braces as a business expense, there's nothing we can do. Tax coaching is about giving you a plan for minimizing your taxes. What should you do? When should you do it? How should you do it?

Tax planning gives you two more powerful advantages.

First, it's the key to your financial defenses. As a business owner, you have two ways to put cash in your pocket. Financial *offense* is making more. Financial *defense* is spending less. For most of us, taxes are our biggest expense. So it makes sense to focus our financial defense where we spend the most. Sure, you can save 15% on car insurance by switching to GEICO, but how much will that really save in the long run?

And second, tax planning guarantees results. You can spend all sorts of time, effort, and money promoting your business, but that can't guarantee results. Or you can set up a medical expense reimbursement plan, deduct your daughter's braces, and guarantee savings.

Let's start by taking a quick look at how the tax system works. This will "lay a foundation" for understanding the specific strategies we'll be talking about soon.

The process starts with income. And this includes most of what you'd think the IRS is interested in:

- Earned income from wages, salaries, bonuses, and commissions
- Profits and losses from your own business
- Interest and dividends from bank accounts, stocks, bonds, and mutual funds
- Capital gains from property sales
- Pensions, IRAs, and annuity income
- Alimony and gambling winning

Even illegal income is taxable. The IRS doesn't care how you make it; the service just wants its share! (The good news is that if you're operating an illegal business, you can deduct the same expenses as if you were running a legitimate business. If you're a bookie, you can deduct the cost of the cell phone you use to take bets.)

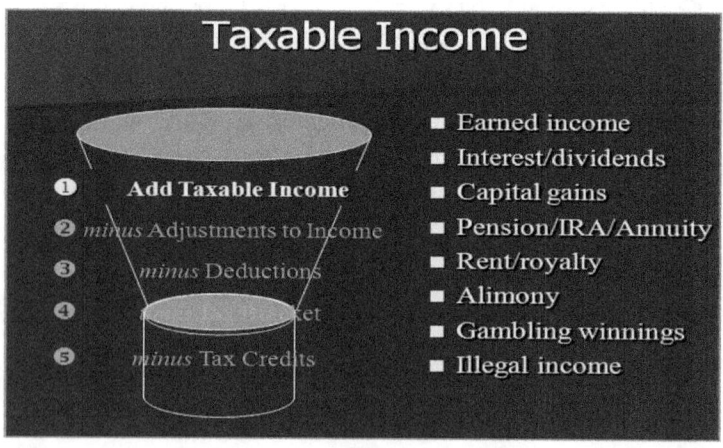

Once you've added up total income, it's time to start sub-tracting "adjustments to income." These are a group of special deductions, listed on the first page of Form 1040, that you can take whether you itemize deductions or not. Total income minus adjustments to income equals "adjusted gross income" or "AGI." Adjustments to income are also called "above the line" deductions, because you take them "above" AGI.

Adjustments include IRA contributions, moving expenses, half of your self-employment tax, self-employed health insurance, self-employed retirement plan contributions, alimony you pay, and student loan interest.

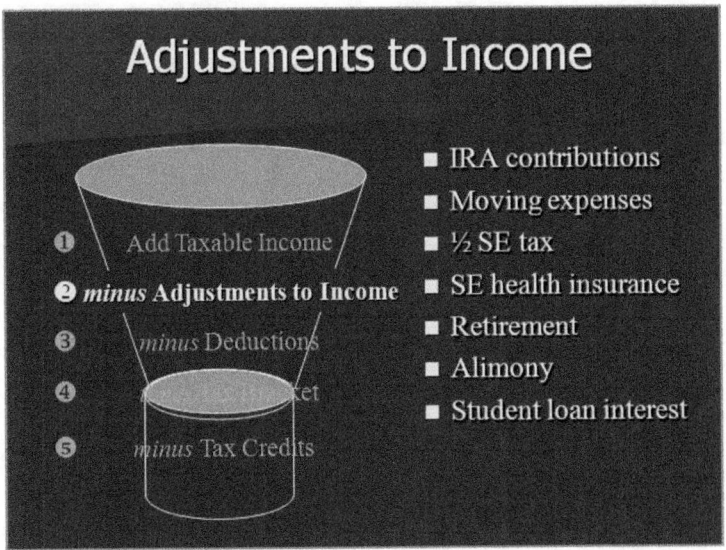

Once you've determined adjusted gross income, you can take a standard deduction or itemized deductions, whichever is greater.

The standard deduction for 2013 is $6,100 for single taxpayers, $8,850 for heads of households, $12,200 for joint filers, and $6,100 each for married couples filing separately.

Tax deductions reduce your taxable income. If you're in the 15% bracket, an extra dollar of deductions cuts your tax by 15 cents. If you're in the 35% bracket, that same extra dollar of deductions cuts your tax by 35 cents.

You can also deduct a personal exemption of $3,900 for yourself, your spouse, and all dependents not claimed by others.

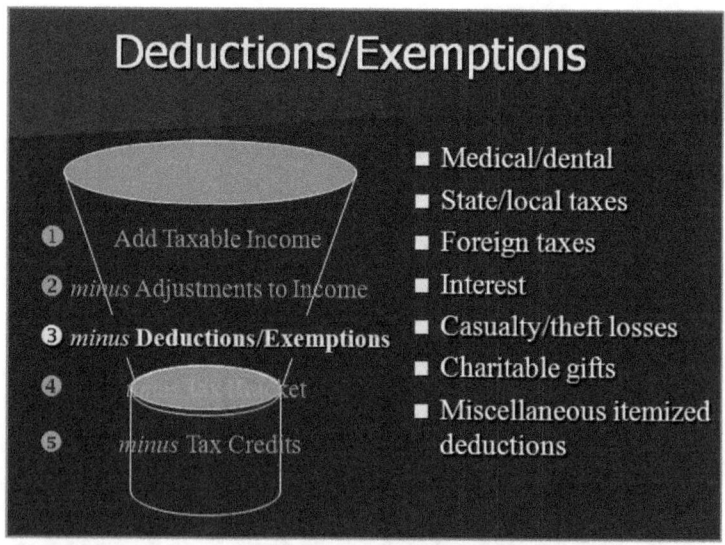

Once you've subtracted deductions and personal exemptions, you'll have taxable income. At that point, the table of tax brackets tells you how much to pay.

You may also owe self-employment tax, which replaces Social Security and Medicare for sole proprietors, partnerships, and LLCs. You'll also owe state and local income and earnings taxes.

Some types of income aren't taxed at the regular rate. For example, tax on "qualified corporate dividends" and on long-term capital gains is capped at 20%.

Also, starting in 2013, there's a 3.8% "unearned income Medicare contribution" on investment income for single taxpayers earning more than $200,000 and joint filers earning more than $250,000. For purposes of this new rule, "investment income" includes interest, dividends, capital gains, rental income, royalties, and annuity distributions.

Finally, you'll subtract any tax credits. These are dollar-for-dollar tax reductions, regardless of your tax bracket. So if you're in the 15% bracket, a dollar's worth of tax credit cuts your tax by a full dollar. If you're in the 35% bracket, an extra dollar's worth of tax credit cuts your tax by the same dollar.

There's no secret to tax credits, other than knowing what's out there. It's worth mentioning at this point that many of the Obama administration's tax proposals involve tax credits, so these will likely become an even more important part of your tax planning.

Ultimately, there are two kinds of dollars in this world: pre-tax dollars and after-tax dollars. Pretax dollars are great. And after-tax dollars aren't bad, but they're not as good as pretax dollars.

So here's the bottom line: You lose every time you spend after-tax dollars that could have been pretax dollars. Let me repeat that. You lose...every time you spend after-tax dollars... that could have been pretax dollars. So how do you turn after-tax dollars into pretax dollars?

There are three primary strategies:

First, earn as much nontaxable income as possible.

Second, make the most of adjustments to income, deductions, and credits. There's really no magic to it other than knowing what's available. Tax planning is excellent for this!

Finally, shift income to later tax years and lower-bracket taxpayers. This includes making the most of tax-deferred retirement plans and shifting income to lower-bracket children, grandchildren, and other family members.

CHAPTER 2

MISTAKE #2:
AUDIT PARANOIA

"The income tax created more criminals than any other single act of government."

BARRY GOLDWATER

ANOTHER day, another IRS scandal. First they were called out for scrutinizing Tea Party organizations and other conservative groups applying for 501(c)(4) status like parents sniffing their teenage son's breath for alcohol. Now they're busted for hosting a lavish $4 million conference featuring *Star Trek* and *Gilligan's Island* video parodies costing $60,000. What's an honest, hardworking, revenue agent to do?

Most of my clients don't like the IRS. Some of them fear the service; others literally hate it with the white-hot intensity of a thousand suns. So how can we as practitioners help our clients really understand the service and what it does? How can we give you some insight on reducing your chance of being audited?

You might fear that aggressive deductions wave flags in front of IRS auditors. But in truth, today's historically low audit rates mean that your odds of attracting attention are slim. And if you've properly documented legitimate deductions, you have little to fear. Audits peaked in 1972 at one out of every forty-four returns. As of 2010, the rate has dropped to one out of every one hundred. Roughly half focused on a single issue: the Earned Income Tax Credit claimed by roughly one in seven filers. (This explains high audit rates for incomes under $25,000.)

The IRS focuses the rest of its efforts on three main targets:

1. Small businesses, particularly sole proprietors operating cash businesses that underreport income and skim receipts. (These make up the bulk of audit targets.)

2. Individual taxpayers who fail to report pass-through income from partnerships, limited liability companies, S corporations, trusts, and estates. (In 2002, the IRS launched a program matching income from those sources to recipients.)

3. Phony trusts, churches, home-based businesses, and similar frauds and protests. (These account for most tax prosecutions—and while the IRS has lost a couple of high-profile criminal prosecutions, no court has upheld any of these tax strategies)

The table below, taken from the 2009–2011 IRS Data Books, summarizes audit data for those years:

Filer	FY 2009	FY 2010	FY 2011
Form 1040 (by "Total Positive Income")			
$0–$199,999	0.7%	1.0%	1.1%
$200,000–$999,999	2.6%	2.7%	3.3%
$1,000,000 +	6.4%	8.4%	12.5%
Schedule C (by Gross Receipts)			
$0–$24,999	1.1%	1.2%	1.3%
$25,000–$99,999	1.9%	2.5%	2.9%
$100,00+	4.2%	4.1%	4.1%
C Corp. (Form 1120)	1.3%	1.4%	1.5%
S Corp. (Form 1120S)	0.4%	0.4%	0.4%
Partnerships (Form 1065)	0.4%	0.4%	0.4%

"Audit-proofing" your return means documenting deductions so that you can prove their validity if you're audited. Today's historically low audit rates mean that it pays to be aggressive. Don't think of "aggressive" as illegal. Aggressive means using all legal tax deductions and loopholes.

But you should file your return as if you expect to be audited. That way, if it happens, you can support your deductions and walk away a winner.

The key to audit defense is proactive tax planning. That means reviewing your taxes *before* year's end to make sure you are using every legal deduction and loophole possible. Remember, tax preparation is not the same as tax planning.

The IRS generally doesn't require records in specific forms (except for travel, entertainment, automobiles, and gifts).[1] To verify expenses, you need to show how much you paid and proof that you paid it.[2] Canceled checks (front and back) and credit card slips can verify payments. If you don't have a check or card slip, you can verify payment with "highly legible" bank statements.[3]

- **Checks** must show the check number, amount, payee, and date it was posted to the account.
- **Electronic funds transfers** must show the amount transferred, the payee's name, and the date the transfer was posted to the account.
- **Credit cards** must show the amount charged, the payee's name, and the transaction date.

---

1   IRS Pub. 552, page 2 (2008).
2   IRS Pub. 552, page 3 (2008).
3   IRS Pub. 552, page 3 (2008).

If you're self-employed or you own a business, your real challenge is proving the business purpose of your expense. The solution is to keep detailed written records, which you can do right in your regular appointment book. This verifies deductions for car and truck expenses,[4] meals and entertainment,[5] home office,[6] business property use,[7] and more. Keep records as close to daily as possible.[8]

Julie Morgenstern, author of *Organizing from the Inside Out*, suggests archiving tax documents in a rotating six-year file: "Outfit a banker's box with six box-bottom file folders labeled Years 1 through 6 (rather than by the year itself to avoid having to relabel annually). Keep last year's tax records and related receipts in the Year 1 folder, the previous year's records in Year 2, and so on. At the end of each year, toss the contents of the bottom folder (Year 6), move each set of records back one folder, and put the records from the year just ended into the folder marked Year 1."

---

4 IRS Pub. 463, page 25 (2008).

5 Reg. §1.274–5(b)(3).

6 IRS Pub. 587, page 16 (2008).

7 IRC §§274(d)(4); 280F.

8 Regs. §1.274–5T(c)(1).

CHAPTER 3

MISTAKE #3:
SELECTING THE WRONG
BUSINESS ENTITY

"Capital punishment: the income tax."

JEFF HAYES

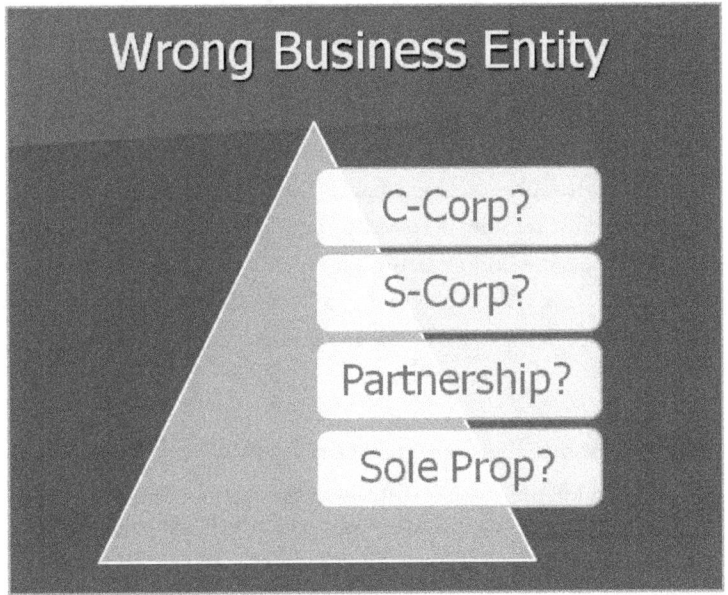

Wrong Business Entity

C-Corp?

S-Corp?

Partnership?

Sole Prop?

THE next mistake is choosing the wrong business entity. One of the most frequent questions I get is, "What business entity should I be?" This question is almost like asking me what should you put in your grocery bag. Most business owners start as sole proprietors; then, as they grow, they establish a limited liability company or corporation to help protect them from business liability. But choosing the right business entity involves all sorts of tax considerations as well. And many business owners are operating with entities that may have been appropriate when they were established, but just don't work as effectively now.

Choosing which entity to operate your business involves two fundamental choices: (1) Will you remain personally liable for business debts? (2) How will you and your business pay tax?

There's no pat answer, and in many cases you'll want more than one entity. Consider these options as starting points:

- **Proprietorship:** This is a business you operate yourself, in your own name or trade name, with no partners or formal entity. You remain personally liable for business debts. You report income and expenses on your personal return and pay income and self-employment tax on your profits. These are best for start-ups and small businesses with no employees in industries with little legal liability.

- **Partnership:** This is an association of two or more partners. General partners (GPs) run the business and remain liable for partnership debts. Limited partners (LPs) invest capital but don't actively manage the business and aren't liable for debts. The partnership files an informational return and passes income and expenses to partners. GP distributions are taxed as ordinary income and are subject to self-employment tax; LP distributions are taxed as passive income.

- **C Corporation:** This is a separate legal entity organized under state law. Your liability for business debts is generally limited to your investment in the corporation. The corporation files its own return, pays tax on profits, and chooses whether or not to pay dividends. Your salary is subject to income and employment tax; dividends are taxed at preferential rates. These are best for owners who need limited liability and want the broadest range of benefits.

- **S Corporation:** This is a corporation that elects not to pay tax itself. Instead, it files an informational return and passes income and losses through to shareholders according to their ownership. Your salary is subject to income and employment tax; pass-through profits are subject to ordinary income tax but not employment tax. These are best for businesses whose owners are active in the business and don't need to accumulate capital for day-to-day operations.

- **Limited Liability Company (LLC):** This is an association of one or more "members" organized under state law. Your liability for business debts is limited to your investment in the company, and LLCs may offer the strongest asset protection of any entity. Single-member LLCs are taxed as proprietors, unless you elect to be taxed as a corporation. Multimember LLCs choose to be taxed as partnerships or corporations. This flexibility and asset-protection strength makes LLCs the entity of choice for many new businesses.

I can't make you an expert in business entities. But I do want to walk through one popular choice to illustrate how important this question can be.

If you operate your business as a sole proprietorship or as a single-member LLC taxed as a sole proprietorship, you may pay as much in self-employment tax as you do in income tax. If that's the case, you might consider setting up an S corporation to reduce that tax.

If you're taxed as a sole proprietor, you'll report your net income on Schedule C. You'll pay tax at whatever your personal rate is. But you'll also pay self-employment tax of 15.3% on your first $113,700 of "net self-employment income" and 2.9% of anything above that. Starting in 2013, you'll also pay a new 0.9% surtax on anything above $200,000 if you're single, $250,000 if you're married filing jointly, or $125,000 if you're married filing separately.

Let's say your profit at the end of the year is $80,000. You'll pay regular tax at your regular rate, whatever that is. You'll also pay about $11,000 in self-employment tax.

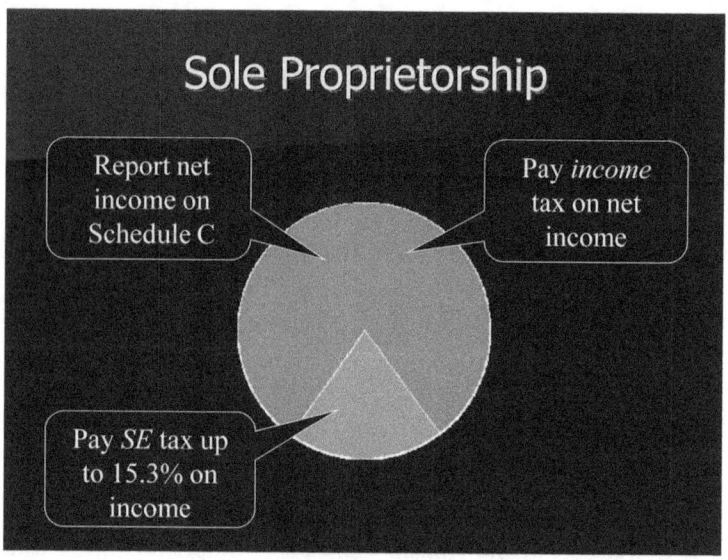

An S corporation is a special corporation that's taxed like a partnership. The corporation pays you a reasonable wage for the work you do. If there's any profit left over, it passes through to you, and you pay the tax on that income on your own return. So the S corporation splits the owner's income into two parts: wages and pass-through distributions. Here's why the S corporation is so attractive:

You'll pay the same 15.3% tax on your wages as you would on your self-employment income, BUT there's no Social Security or self-employment tax due on the dividend pass-through.

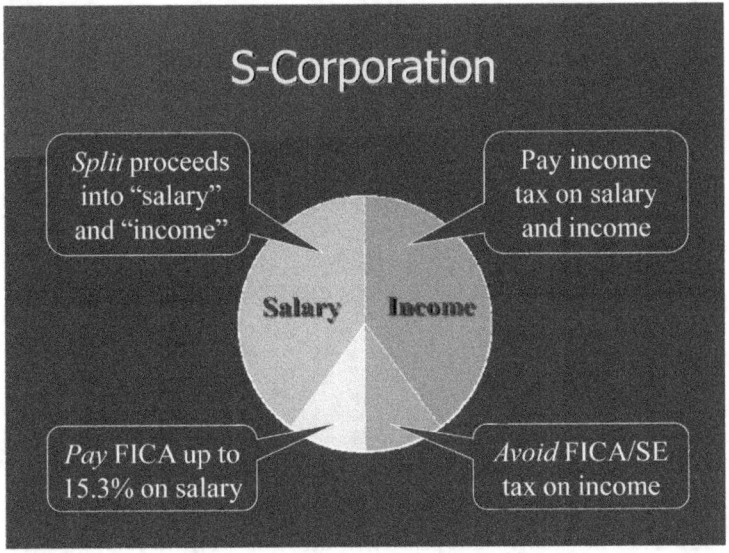

Let's say your S corporation earns the same $80,000 as your proprietorship. If you pay yourself $40,000 in wages, you'll pay about $6,120 in Social Security, but you'll avoid employment tax on the income distribution.

And that *saves* you $5,184 in employment tax you would have paid without the S corporation.

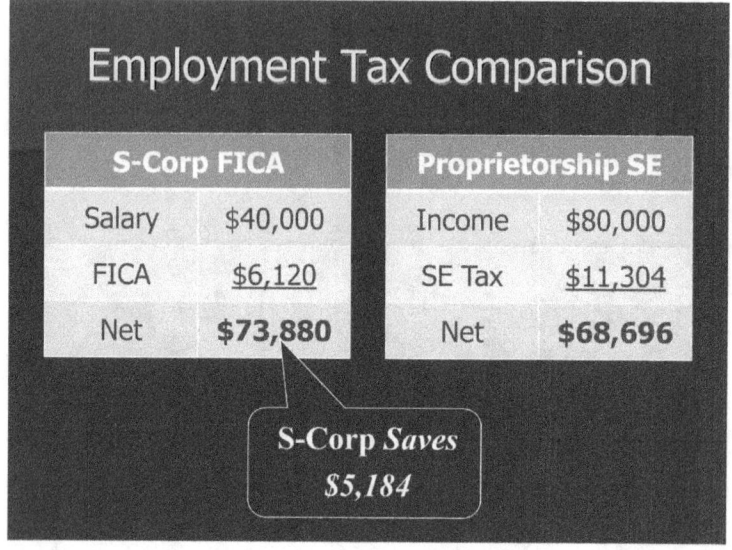

I caution my clients that they must pay themselves a reasonable salary. If you are making $1 million a year, a $50,000 annual salary is too low. I also remind my clients that their Social Security income base will be lower. That is why I recommend that they take the savings and put them into a retirement account over which *they* will have control.

CHAPTER 4

MISTAKE #4:
SELECTING THE WRONG
RETIREMENT PLAN

"For every benefit you receive a tax is levied."

RALPH WALDO EMERSON

#4: Wrong Retirement Plan

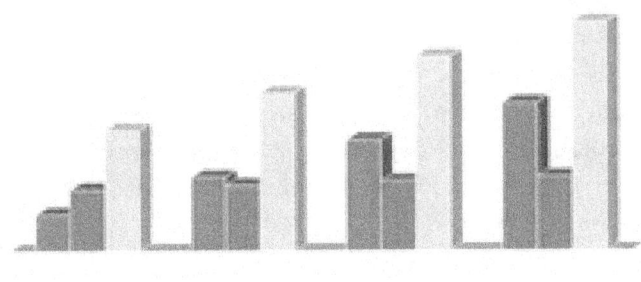

So many business owners pour their hearts and souls into their company. When companies are first started, there typically is not enough money to save for retirement. I don't like to use the word "retirement"; I like to say "saving for the day when working is optional." Nevertheless, you should always save money for the day when you are not working.

My motto is, "Pay yourself first." Why do I say that? The next time you get your paycheck stub, take a look to see who takes out their money first. It is the IRS! With a retirement plan, you can set it up so that you get paid first from your retirement savings deduction. Isn't that better than paying the IRS first?

Now let's talk about the fourth mistake: choosing the wrong retirement plan. If you're looking to save more than the $5,500 limit for IRAs, you have three main choices: Simplified employee pensions (SEPs), SIMPLE IRAs, or 401(k)s.

This book will not make you an expert on retirement plans. But I *can* help you decide pretty quickly if the plan you have is right for you or whether you should be looking for something more suited to your specific needs. So bear with me, even if the next few illustrations look intimidating. These are some very powerful strategies.

The SEP is the easiest plan to set up because it's just a turbo-charged IRA:

- If you're self-employed, you can contribute up to 25% of your "net self-employment income."
- If your business is incorporated and you're salaried, you can contribute 25% of your "covered compensation," which is roughly the same as your salary.
- The maximum contribution for 2013 is $51,000.
- If you've got employees, you'll have to contribute for them too. You generally have to contribute the same percentage for your employees as you do for yourself. However, you can use what's called an "integrated" formula to make extra contributions for higher incomes.
- The money goes straight into employee IRA accounts. There's no annual administration or paperwork required.

The SEP is easy to adopt, easy to maintain, and flexible. If there's no money to contribute, you just don't contribute. But the contribution is limited to a percentage of your income. If you set up an S corporation to limit self-employment tax, you'll also limit your SEP contribution.

The next step up the retirement plan ladder is the SIMPLE IRA. This is another "turbocharged" IRA that lets you contribute more than the usual $5,500 limit:

- You and your employees can contribute up to $12,000. If you're fifty or older you can make an extra $2,500 "catch-up" contribution. If your income is under $48,000, that may be more than you could sock away with an SEP. (That's because $12,000 is *more than* 25% of whatever you could contribute to an SEP.)
- But you have to match everyone's deferral or make profit-sharing contributions. You can match everyone's contribution dollar-for-dollar up to 3% of their pay or contribute 2% of everyone's pay whether they defer or not. If you choose the match, you can reduce it as low as 1% for two years out of five.
- Money goes straight into employee IRAs. You can designate a single financial institution to hold the money, or you can let your employees choose.
- Like the SEP, there's no setup charge or annual administration fee.

The SIMPLE IRA may be best for part-time or sideline businesses earning less than $48,000. You can also hire your spouse or children, and they can make SIMPLE contributions.

The final step up the ladder is the 401(k). Most people think of 401(k)s as retirement plans for bigger businesses. But you can set up what's called a "solo" or "individual" 401(k) just for yourself.

The 401(k) is a true "qualified" plan. This means you'll set up a trust, adopt a written plan agreement, and choose a trustee. But the 401(k) lets you contribute far more money and have far more flexibility than either the SEP or the SIMPLE.

- You and your employees can "defer" 100% of your income up to $17,500. If you're fifty or older, you can make an extra $5,500 "catch-up" contribution.
- You can choose to match your employees' contributions, or you can make profit-sharing contributions up to 25% of their pay. That's the same percentage you can save in your SEP—on top of the $17,500 deferral.
- The maximum contribution for 2013 is $51,000 per person, plus any "catch-up" contributions.
- You can offer yourself and your employees loans, hardship withdrawals, and all the bells and whistles "the big boys" offer their employees.
- 401(k)s are generally more difficult to administer. There are antidiscrimination rules to keep you from stuffing your own account while you stiff your employees. If you operate your business by yourself, you can establish an "individual" 401(k) with less red tape, and it is easy to administer. And again, you can hire your spouse and contribute to his or her account.

If you're older and you want to contribute more than the $51,000 limit for SEPs or 401(k)s, consider a traditional defined benefit pension plan:

- Defined benefit plans let you guarantee up to $205,000 in annual income.

- You can contribute—and deduct—as much as you need to finance that benefit. You'll calculate those contributions according to your age, your desired retirement age, your current income, and various actuarial factors.
- A 412(i) plan, which is funded entirely with life insurance or annuities, lets you contribute even more.
- Defined benefit plans have required annual contributions. But you can combine a defined benefit plan with a 401(k) or SEP to give yourself a little more flexibility.

I had a couple that came to me for advice about their retirement plan. They felt they were not saving enough and were not sure what to do or where the money would come from. After doing a tax plan for the couple, I freed up about $18,000 in annual tax savings by implementing one of our common tax strategies. With the extra cash flow, they opened a "solo" 401(k) plan. They decided to add another $12,000 to their retirement savings for a total of $30,000 per year. After ten years, that is $300,000! And that does not even include growth on the account.

As you grow with your business, your retirement plan needs change as well. If you can combine tax planning with financial planning, you may come up with extra tax savings that can be used for the retirement planning. It is very important that the tax and financial planning be done in unison. That is one of the reasons my firm offers both. I do hear from many clients that their accountant and financial planner never meet with each other, and I see many cases of missed opportunities. As Frank Sinatra famously sang, "You can't have one without the other."

CHAPTER 5

MISTAKE #5:
MISSING FAMILY
EMPLOYMENT

"Taxation with representation ain't so hot either."

GERALD BARZAN

#5: Missing Family Employment

- Children age 7+
- First $6,100 tax-free
- Next $8,950 taxed at 10%
- "Reasonable" wages
- Written job description, timesheet, check
- Account in child's name
- FICA/FUTA savings

NOW let's talk about the fifth mistake: missing family employment. Hiring your children and grandchildren can be a great way to cut taxes on your income by shifting it to someone who pays less in taxes than you do.

- Yes, there's a minimum age. They have to be at least seven years old.
- Their first $6,100 of earned income is taxed at zero. That's because it's the standard deduction for a single taxpayer, even if you claim them as your dependent. Their next $8,950 is taxed at just 10%, so you can shift a lot of income downstream.
- You have to pay them a "reasonable" wage for the service they perform. The tax court says that a "reasonable wage" is what you'd pay a commercial vendor for the same service, with an

adjustment made for the child's age and experience. So, if your twelve-year-old son cuts grass for your rental properties, pay him what a landscaping service might charge. If your fifteen-year-old helps keep your books, pay him a bit less than a bookkeeping service might charge. Does anyone have a teenager who helps with your website? What would you pay a commercial designer for that service?

- To audit-proof your return, write out a job description and keep a time sheet.
- Pay by check so you can document the payment.
- You have to deposit the check into an account in the child's name. But it doesn't have to be his pizza-and-Nintendo fund. It can be a Roth IRA for decades of tax-free growth. It can be a section 529 college savings plan. Or it can be a custodial account that you control until she turns twenty-one. Now you can't use money in a custodial account for your obligations of parental support. But private and parochial school aren't obligations of parental support. Sleep-away summer camp isn't an obligation of parental support.

Let's say your teenage daughter wants to spend two weeks at horse camp. You can earn the fee yourself, pay tax on it, and pay for camp with after-tax dollars. Or you can pay her to work in your business, deposit the check in her custodial account, and then, as custodian, write a check to the camp. Hiring your daughter effectively lets you deduct her camp as a business expense.

If you hire your child to work in an unincorporated business, you don't have to withhold for Social Security until he turns eighteen. So this really is tax-free money. You'll have to issue your child a W-2 at the end of the year, but this is painless compared to the tax you'll waste if you don't take advantage of this strategy.

As a business owner myself, I have employed all five of my children. During the college years it allowed me to save money on taxes that I could use for college expenses. College is very expensive these days, and every penny saved helps!

Another great way to shift income is to pay your parents. Let's say you are supporting your parents financially. If you own a business, why not pay them to perform certain functions for your business? This allows you to deduct the expense through your business. Your parents will have to pay income tax on their salaries, but it could be at a much lower rate.

CHAPTER 6

MISTAKE #6:
MISSING MEDICAL
DEDUCTIONS

"The United States has a system
of taxation by confession."

HUGO BLACK

NOW let's talk about health-care costs. Surveys once showed that taxes *used to be* small business owners' biggest concern. Now it's rising health-care costs. If you pay for your own health insurance, you can deduct it as an adjustment to income on page 1 of Form 1040. If you itemize deductions, you can deduct unreimbursed medical and dental expenses on Schedule A, *if* they total more than 10% (7.5% over age sixty-five) of your adjusted gross income. But most of us don't spend that much. What if there was a way to write off medical bills as business expenses? There is—it's called a Medical Expense Reimbursement Plan (MERP), or section 105 Plan.[9]

This is an employee benefit plan, which means it requires an employee. If you operate your business as a sole proprietorship, partnership, LLC, or S corporation, you're considered self-employed. So if you're married, hire your spouse. If you're not married, you can do this with a C corporation. But you don't have to be incorporated. You can do it as a sole proprietor or LLC by hiring your spouse. The one exception is the S corporation. If you own more than 2% of the stock, you and your spouse are both considered self-employed for purposes of this rule. You'll need to use another source of income, not taxed as an S Corporation as the basis for this plan.

If you hire your spouse to qualify for a MERP, you can pay him or her in benefits only rather than cash. This avoids managing payroll formalities and filing Form W-2. The key to making this work is to document your spouse's bona fide employment. Consider executing a written employment contract. Track your

---

9   IRC §105(b).

spouse's hours, weekly or monthly, to substantiate your deduction. You'll also need to pay expenses out of the business (or show actual reimbursements to employees) and show that he or she is receiving "reasonable compensation" for the work your employee-spouse performs.

Plan benefits are deductible by the business and nontaxable to the employee. Here's how they work:

- You have to establish the plan for employees. If you run your business as a proprietorship, partnership, LLC, or S corporation, you're considered "self-employed" and not eligible.[10] If you're single, you can establish a C corporation and pay benefits to yourself as an employee. If you're married, you can hire your spouse and pay the benefits through him or her.[11] If you operate as an S corporation, you and your spouse are both considered self-employed (in that case, segregate part of your income through a proprietorship or C corporation and pay benefits through that entity).
- You can't discriminate in favor of highly compensated employees.[12] However, you can use a classification test (such as "all participants in employer's group health plan") to qualify participants.[13] You can also exclude those under age twenty-five, those who regularly work less than thirty-five hours per week, those who work less than nine months out

---

10 IRC §105(g).
11 Rev. Rul. 71-558; PLR 9409006.
12 IRC §105(h)(2).
13 IRC §105(h)(3)(A)(ii).

of the year, and those who have worked for you for less than three years.[14]

- You can't reimburse employees for costs they incur before the plan effective date.[15] Paying medical expenses through a MERP offers several advantages:

  ☐ You can deduct 100% of your employees' health insurance. Deductible health insurance costs include major medical and supplemental premiums, Medicare premiums, qualified long-term care premiums, and Medicare supplemental ("Medigap") policies.

  ☐ Out-of-pocket medical costs include routine expenses such as co-pays, deductibles, and prescriptions; occasional expenses such as eyeglasses and dentistry; and big-ticket items like orthodontics, fertility treatments, and schools for learning-disabled children.[16] It also includes over-the-counter medicines and health-care supplies, if prescribed by a physician.[17] You can reimburse employees or pay health-care providers directly.[18]

  ☐ The plan lets you deduct 100% of your out-of-pocket costs, bypassing the usual 10% floor for itemized deductions. You'll also avoid any self-employment tax you would otherwise pay on amounts you deduct as plan benefits.

---

14 IRC §105(h)(3)(9B); Regs. §1.105-11(c)(2)(iii).
15 Rev. Rul. 2002-58.
16 IRC §105(b).
17 IRS Notice 2011-5.
18 IRC §105(b) ("...amounts are paid, directly or indirectly...").

If a medical expense reimbursement plan isn't appropriate, consider the new Health Savings Accounts. I often use these plans for sole owners of S corporations. These arrangements combine a high-deductible health plan with a tax-free savings account to cover unreimbursed costs.

To qualify, you'll need a high-deductible health plan with a deductible of at least $1,250 for single coverage or $2,500 for family coverage. Neither you nor your spouse can be covered by a non-high-deductible health plan or Medicare. The plan can't provide any benefit, other than certain preventive care benefits, until the deductible for that year is satisfied. You're not eligible if you're covered by a separate plan or rider offering prescription drug benefits before the minimum annual deductible is satisfied. Once you've established your eligibility, you can open a deductible savings account.

Health Savings Account

1. "High deductible health plan"
   - $1,250+ deductible (individual coverage)
   - $2,500+ deductible (family coverage)

Plus

2. Tax-deductible "Health Savings Account"
   - Contribute & deduct up to $3,250/$6,450 per year
   - Account grows tax-free
   - Tax-free withdrawals for qualified expenses

You can contribute up to $3,250 for singles or $6,450 for families. You can use it for most kinds of health insurance, including COBRA continuation and long-term care premiums. You can also use it for the same sort of expenses as a section 105 plan.

The Health Savings Account isn't as powerful as the section 105 plan. You've got specific dollar contribution limits, and there's no self-employment tax advantage. But Health Savings Accounts can still cut your overall health-care costs.

As stated in chapter 3, the choice of entity for your business should not be selected for legal reasons alone. If you have high medical expenses, your choice of business entity could be a big factor on whether you can write them off or not. It all comes down to tax planning to make sure you are getting the most out of your deductions.

CHAPTER 7

MISTAKE #7: MISSING HOME OFFICE EXPENSES

"Count the day won when, turning on its axis,
This earth imposes no additional taxes."

FRANKLIN P. ADAMS

THE home office deduction is probably the most misunderstood deduction in the entire tax code. For years, taxpayers feared it raised an automatic audit flag. But Congress has relaxed the rules, so now it's far less likely to attract attention.

Your home office qualifies as your principal place of business if (1) you use it "exclusively and regularly for administrative or management activities of your trade or business" and (2) "you have no other fixed location where you conduct substantial administrative or management activities of your trade or business." This is true even if you have another office, so long as you don't use it more than occasionally for administrative or management activities.

You have to use your office regularly and exclusively for business. "Regularly" generally means ten to twelve hours per week. To prove your deduction, keep a log and take photos to record your business use. You can claim a workshop, studio, or "separately identifiable" space you use to store products or samples. The space doesn't have to be an entire room. If you use it for more than one business, both have to qualify to take the deduction.

To calculate your deduction:

1. Determine business use percentage ("BUP") of your home. You can divide by the number of rooms if they're roughly equal, or you can calculate the exact percentage of square footage. Exclude common areas like halls and stairs to boost BUP.
2. Deduct BUP of rent, mortgage interest, and property taxes.

3. Depreciate the BUP of your home's basis (excluding land) over thirty-nine years as nonresidential property.
4. Deduct BUP of utilities, repairs, insurance, garbage pickup, and security. If BUP for specific expenses differs from BUP for the home (such as high electric bills for home office equipment), claim the difference as "direct" expenses.

You can use home office expenses to shelter profits, but not below zero. If home office expenses exceed your net business income, carry forward excess losses to future years.

When you sell your home, you'll have to report any depreciation you claimed or could have claimed after May 6, 1997, as "unrecaptured section 1250 gain." You can still claim the $500,000 tax-free exclusion for home office space unless it's a "separate dwelling unit."

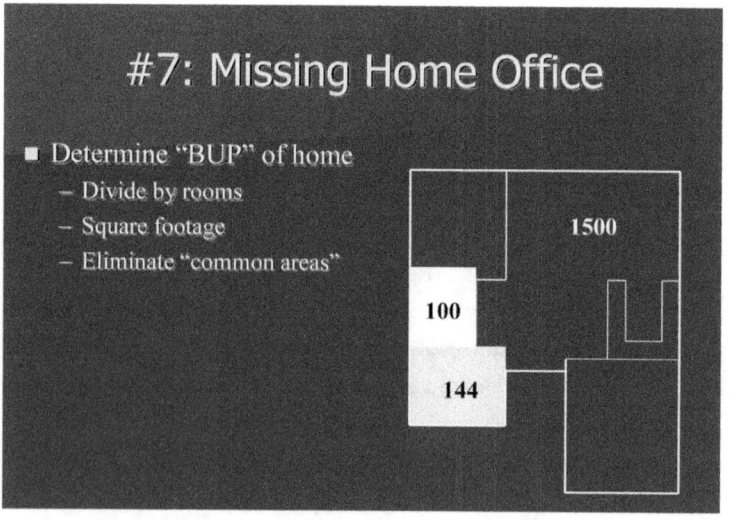

Starting in 2013, you can use a "safe harbor" method to deduct $5 per square foot, for up to three hundred square feet of qualifying office space. You'll continue to deduct your mortgage

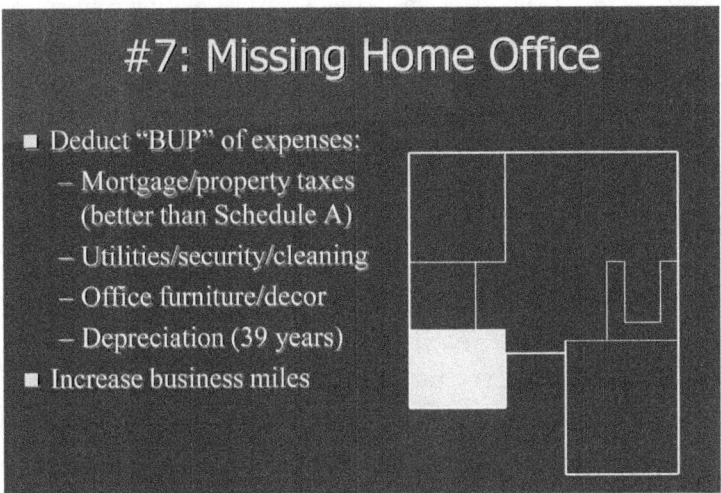

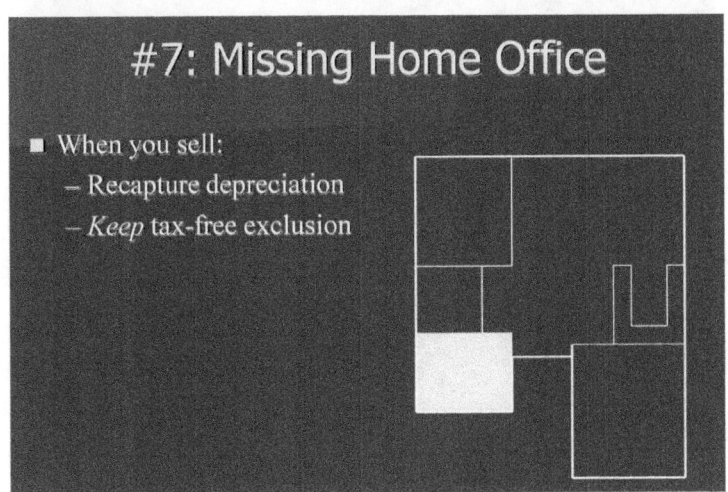

interest and property tax on Schedule A. However, you'll forgo any depreciation deduction.

On a separate note, code section 280A(g) lets you rent your home tax free for up to fourteen days. Consider renting your entire home to your business for meetings, entertainment, or similar purposes to deduct money from your business without owing tax on it personally.

For example, you hold business meetings, holiday parties, and board meetings at your home for a total of fourteen days. You then charge your company the going rate for the space. If you own an expensive home, this could be a substantial write-off for your business. Better yet, you don't have to personally claim the income. Remember, you can use this even if you do not claim a home office deduction.

CHAPTER 8

MISTAKE #8:
MISSING AUTO
AND TRUCK EXPENSES

"The nation should have a tax system that looks
like someone designed it on purpose."

WILLIAM SIMON

NOW let's look at car and truck expenses. I don't want to take too much space on this, but I do want to point out the most common mistake clients make with these expenses.

Let me remind you that the current mileage deduction is 56.5 cents per mile. So my question to you is what kind of vehicle do you drive and how much do you deduct? Are you detecting a pattern here? That deduction is the same for everyone, no matter what we drive. Do you think we all spend the same to operate our cars? It might surprise you to see how much it really costs to operate your car. And it's *not* exactly 56.5 cents per mile!

Every year, the American Automobile Association (AAA) publishes a vehicle operating-cost survey. Costs vary according to how much you drive, but if you're taking the standard deduction for a car that costs more than 56.5 cents per mile, you're losing money every time you turn the key. If you're taking the standard deduction now, you can switch to the "actual expense" method if you own your car, but not if you lease.

You can't switch from actual expenses to the mileage allowance if you've taken accelerated depreciation. Car and truck expenses for trips on behalf of your trade or business are a deductible business expense. Your first step involves calculating your business use percentage (BUP) for your vehicle. The IRS divides mileage into three categories: (1) business, (2) commuting, and (3) personal. Ordinary commuting and personal trips are nondeductible. Trips from home to your first business stop and trips from your last business stop to home are personal. (Daily trips to the bank, post office, and similar stops where you perform no service don't qualify.)

Travel between temporary business stops is deductible. So, for example, if you leave home, make six business stops, meet a prospect for dinner, then drive home, your mileage between your first stop and the restaurant is deductible. However, if you have a regular business stop (one that you make at least eight to ten times in a six-month period) that you expect to last less than a year, you can count those as business miles too. (1) If home is your principal place of business, then all business trips are deductible. (2) Once you've calculated your BUP, you have two ways to calculate your deduction:

- The mileage allowance is 56.50 cents per mile (2013) *plus* parking, tolls, and your BUP of interest on your car loan and state and local personal property tax on the vehicle.
- With "actual expenses," deduct your BUP of all expenses:
  - ❑ Depreciation and interest (purchased vehicles)
  - ❑ Lease payments (leased vehicles)
  - ❑ Insurance
  - ❑ Gasoline, oil, and car washes
  - ❑ Tires, maintenance, and repairs
  - ❑ Licenses, tags, and personal property tax
  - ❑ Parking and tolls
- The allowance for charitable use of the vehicle is capped at just 14 cents per mile, and for medical and moving use, 24 cents per mile.

Don't assume that easier record keeping justifies settling for the "one size fits all" allowance. It's the same for every vehicle, no matter how big or expensive. And the wrong choice can cost you thousands. The AAA estimates that 2012 actual costs per mile exceeded the IRS flat rate in almost all categories of vehicles and driving habits, at a gasoline cost of $3.36 a gallon.

If you own rather than lease your car, you can switch from the allowance to actual expenses. You'll have to use straight-line, rather than accelerated, depreciation. You can't go the other direction, switching from actual expenses to the allowance, if you've claimed any first-year expensing or accelerated depreciation.

CHAPTER 9

MISTAKE #9:
MISSING MEALS, TRAVEL, AND ENTERTAINMENT EXPENSES

"A person doesn't know how much he has to be thankful for until he has to pay taxes on it."

AUTHOR UNKNOWN

MEALS and entertainment are two of my favorite things in life. Add in the fact that you can deduct part of it for taxes, and it makes it even yummier. The basic rule is that you can deduct cost for meals with a bona fide business purpose. This means clients, prospects, referral sources, and business colleagues. And let me ask you: when do you ever eat with someone who's not a client, prospect, referral source, or business colleague? If you're in a business like real estate, insurance, or investments where you're marketing yourself, the answer might be "never." Be as aggressive as you can with what you define as bona fide business discussions!

The general rule is that you can deduct 50% of your meals and entertainment, so long as it isn't "lavish or extraordinary." The IRS knows you have to eat, so you can't deduct it all. But they'll meet you halfway. How many of you entertain at home? Do you ever discuss business? Are you deducting those meals too? There's no requirement that you eat out. Don't forget to deduct home entertainment expenses too! You can deduct entertainment expenses if they take place directly before or after substantial, bona fide discussion directly related to the active conduct of your business. You can deduct the face value of tickets to sporting and theatrical events, food and beverages, parking, taxes, and tips. You can't deduct meals with your spouse unless you're traveling together for business. However, you can include the cost of a spouse or other "closely connected" person (such as children or parents) if your guest brings *his* or *her* spouse. If your spouse is an employee or shareholder, then you can deduct his or her share of the expense.

#9: Missing Meals/Entertainment

- *Bona fide* business discussion
  - Clients
  - Prospects
  - Referral Sources
  - Business colleagues
- 50% of most expenses
- Home entertainment
- Associated entertainment

You don't need receipts for expenses under $75. But you do need to record five pieces of information in your business diary or records. And you should do it as close to daily as possible. The IRS wants to know (1) the cost of the meal, (2) the date of the meal, (3) the place where it takes place, (4) the business purpose of your discussion, and (5) your business relationship with your guest. There are plenty of new apps that allow you to take a picture of the receipt and send it to your e-mail, or better yet to your credit card statement. After a meal, I write the basics of why the meal was done on the receipt. I scan it, and my credit card company has an app that will link the scanned picture to the charge on the credit card.

Travel costs are different than meals in that the cost associated with business travel should be 100% deductible for trips you take on behalf of your trade or business. Here are some guidelines:

- You're "traveling" when you're away overnight or long enough to need sleep.

- "Business days" are those you spend traveling to business destinations, days where you spend the majority of working hours on your trade or business (four hours and one minute), and days where your personal presence is required at a particular place for a specific and bona fide business purpose.

- "Business day" costs include 50% of meals and entertainment plus 100% of lodging, local transportation, incidentals, and your first load of laundry and dry cleaning back home.

- If your spouse is a bona fide employee traveling for a bona fide business purpose, you can deduct his or her costs.

- Save receipts for all lodging and for any expense over $75.

- Transportation costs include cars, planes, trains, and boats.

Want to write off weekends? You can treat them as business days if they fall between business appointments or you stay over (before or after your business) to qualify for airline "Saturday stay" discounts.

If you travel to find investment property, amortize the cost of the trip over the first sixty months you place the property in service. If you don't find property to buy, deduct the cost of the trip as a business loss.

CHAPTER 10

MISTAKE #10:
NOT USING YOUR BUSINESS TO PAY FOR YOUR KIDS' TUITION

"A fine is a tax for doing something wrong.
A tax is a fine for doing something right."

AUTHOR UNKNOWN

As a parent of three daughters who are in college, I know firsthand the cost of higher education. No matter how much you have saved, it seems to cost more. Add in the expenses of a sorority or fraternity, and the outlay is even higher. Luckily, I own a business and can use my business to create what is known in the tax world as "tax scholarships."

Let me first start out by saying that some business owners' kids will receive no financial aid other than Stafford or Plus loans because of their high level of income. But as stated previously, if you own a business you can use it to your advantage to create business tax breaks. There are many ways to do this, and I will only a cover a few topics in this book.

Income Shifting: As stated in chapter 5, "Missing Family Employment," having your teenage or college-bound kid work for you is a great way to shift income from you to your child, who should be in a lower tax bracket.

Gift-Leaseback: Gift-leasebacks (and sale-leasebacks) let you transfer income from yourself to lower-bracket taxpayers such as your children. You, the donor, give or sell business property to the taxpayers you wish to shift income to or to an irrevocable trust for their benefit (if they are under age eighteen). Then, lease it back from the recipient. This strategy essentially lets you give depreciated property to your kids and deduct it again. Your gift is valued at its fair market value as of the date of the gift. If you give more than $14,000 in a single year to a single donor, you'll need to file a gift tax return; however, no actual tax is payable until your lifetime taxable gifts exceed $5 million. You and your spouse can jointly give $14,001 to $28,000 by consenting in writing to "split" the gift. Once you've made appropriate gifts, follow these rules to qualify for deductions:

- You can't retain substantially the same control over the property you transfer. If you give property to a trust, you can avoid this issue by appointing an independent trustee.
- The lease should be in writing and specify timely payment of reasonable rent. Have the property appraised before transfer and maintain the payment schedule you specify. (You might consider a "net lease" that requires you to pay, and thus deduct, maintenance, repairs, and the like.)
- You'll need to pay commercially reasonable rent.
- You can't retain any disqualifying equity in the property after the lease—preferably, not even a reversionary interest in property gifted in trust.

The gift-leaseback has been especially useful for children age eighteen or above in college or grad school.

Example: You own a fully depreciated SUV you use 100% for business. The truck's fair market value is $20,000. You and your spouse give it to your college-age daughter and lease it back for $400 per month. Your arrangement creates $4,800 in new deductions and eliminates any self-employment tax you would otherwise have paid on that income. But be aware that ever since January 1, 2008, the "kiddie tax" applies to dependents under age nineteen and full-time students under age twenty-four, thus greatly limiting this strategy. This technique is useful for kids in grad school.

Tuition Reimbursement Plan: Education assistance plans let you reimburse employees for undergraduate and graduate level education expenses, whether they are directly related to the employee's job or not. Here's how they work:

- The plan must be a separate written plan for the exclusive benefit of employees.
- You can reimburse up to $5,250 in expenses per employee per year. Reimbursements are deductible by the business and nontaxable to the student.
- Education assistance plans can't pay more than 5% of their total benefits in a year to the employer's owners, spouses, or dependent children. But if your child is age twenty-one or older and you no longer claim him or her as a dependent, your ownership of the business is no longer attributed to them. This means that you can hire your college-age children (under the same rules as for hiring any child) and pay them an extra $5,250, tax-free, for college. (To verify your deduction and audit-proof your return, keep a time sheet showing the dates, hours, and services performed. No payroll or paychecks are required if you pay your child in the form of education assistance plan benefits only.)
- Education assistance plans aren't subject to the Employee Retirement Income Security Act (ERISA). You don't need to establish a trust or pre-fund benefits. You don't need to file Form 5500 or any other prescribed reporting. And you can pay plan benefits out of general assets or day-to-day cash flow.

These are just a few ways you can create a tax scholarship for your college-bound children.

CHAPTER 11

MISTAKE #11: MISSING REAL ESTATE DEDUCTIONS

"Death and taxes may be inevitable, but they shouldn't be related."

J. C. WATTS JR.

VACATION HOMES offer similar tax breaks as your primary residence, plus the chance to earn tax-free rent. Here's how:

- You can deduct mortgage interest you pay on up to $1 million of "acquisition indebtedness" to buy your primary residence and one extra residence. If your mortgage debt tops $1 million, you can still deduct the interest you pay on the first $1 million of acquisition indebtedness. Write off the highest-rate mortgage first to maximize your break.

- You can deduct interest you pay on a loan secured by a time-share, yacht, or motor home so long as it includes sleeping, cooking, and toilet facilities.

- If you rent your home for fourteen days or less, income is tax-free. If you rent your vacation home for more than fourteen days, your rental income is taxable, but your mortgage interest, property taxes, maintenance, utilities, and other expenses can be declared to shelter that income. There are two ways to figure deductible expenses:

1. If you use the home personally for more than the greater of fourteen days or 10% of the rental days, it qualifies as residential property. (Personal use includes days your family uses the house, days you rent it for below market rates, days you trade its use for someplace else, and time you donate as a charitable gift, but not days you use to prepare it for rental.) You'll have to report your income—but your expenses may offset it enough to avoid paying tax. To calculate the

rental portion of mortgage interest and property taxes, divide the days of rental use by 365. For maintenance and utilities, divide the days of rental use by the days of total use (including rental and personal use). You can deduct rental expenses such as advertising, commissions, and travel—but not depreciation. Any losses are nondeductible personal losses.

2. If you use it personally for less than the greater of fourteen days or 10% of rental days, it qualifies as rental property. To calculate the rental portion of your mortgage interest, property taxes, maintenance, and utilities, divide the days of rental use by the days of total use. (There's no separate formula for "empty days" with mortgage interest and property taxes as there is when you treat the home as residential property.) You can deduct rental expenses such as advertising, commissions, and travel. And you can deduct depreciation. If the property generates a loss, you can deduct it against outside income if you qualify for the rental real estate loss allowance or you qualify as a real estate professional.

Rental real estate is ordinarily a "passive" activity unless you are a real estate professional. You can't use passive losses to offset ordinary income. But you can avoid at least part of this restriction if you qualify for the rental real estate loss allowance. If your AGI is $150,000 or less, you can claim up to $25,000 in rental real estate loss allowance from property you "actively participate" in managing. This allowance phases out by 50 cents for each dollar of AGI between $100,000 and $150,000. Here's how it works:

- You have to "actively participate" in managing the property. (You're not treated as actively participating if you own less than

10% by value of the activity or if you participate solely as a limited partner.) Active participation doesn't require regular, continuous, or substantial involvement. You qualify even if your involvement is limited to making management decisions and hiring independent contractors to provide actual services.

- You first have to net out losses against other real estate in which you materially participate, then any other passive income, before claiming the allowance.

- Married couples filing separately can't claim the allowance.

- If your losses are disallowed because your AGI exceeds $100,000, you can carry forward those losses until such time as you can use the allowance or you dispose of the property.

You can't take the allowance for six specific uses treated as businesses rather than rentals:

1. "Incidental" rentals of property, where the main reason for holding the property is to profit from the gain and the rental income is less than 2% of the property's value

2. Short-term rentals averaging seven days or less

3. Rentals averaging between seven and thirty days where the property owner provides significant personal service

4. Rentals involving extraordinary personal service (nursing homes, etc.)

5. Property provided for use by a partnership or corporation not engaged in the business of renting property (such as a taxpayer who provides, but does not actually rent, an office building to a partnership or corporation in which the taxpayer has an ownership interest and actively participates in the business of that entity)

6. Property owned for use of customers during regular business hours (such as a golf course or swimming pool)

Rental real estate is ordinarily a "passive" activity. You can't use passive income as a basis for employee benefits like medical expense reimbursements or retirement plans for yourself. But you can hire your spouse to help manage your properties and establish benefits for him or her.

You can establish plans for employees, but not independent contractors. You're treated as self-employed (and thus *not* an employee) for properties you own yourself, through a partnership or LLC, or through an S corporation. And your spouse is also treated as self-employed, for most employee benefit purposes, for properties he or she owns jointly with you or jointly through a partnership, LLC, or S corporation. If you and your spouse own all your properties jointly, you'll have to choose one of you to give up ownership in one or more properties or entities. The easiest way for you or your spouse to accomplish this is to quitclaim title to actual property or gift your ownership in your partnership, LLC, or S corporation. This is a tax-free transfer; your basis in your interest transfers to your spouse. Keep a time sheet showing your spouse's hours and services. If you pay a salary to qualify your spouse for retirement plan contributions, you'll manage his or her payroll just as you would for any other employee.

Once you've cleared these hurdles and established bona fide employment, you'll qualify for a complete range of employee benefit plans, including section 105 medical expense reimbursements; SIMPLE IRA, 401(k), or other retirement plans; and "certain fringe benefits" available to any employer.

As mentioned previously, rental real estate is ordinarily a "passive" activity. You can't use passive losses to offset ordinary income. However, you can elect not to treat rental activities in which you "materially participate" as passive activities *if* you qualify as a "real estate professional." This lets you deduct your full loss from those activities—not just your first $25,000 and regardless of your overall adjusted gross income. How do you qualify as a real estate professional? You meet the "material participation" test for an activity by participating throughout the year on a regular, continuous, and substantial basis. You can demonstrate this in one of seven ways:

1. You participate for more than five hundred hours.

2. You provide "substantially all" management services.

3. You participate for more than one hundred hours during the tax year, and your participation is not less than that of any other individual (including nonowners) for the year.

4. You "significantly participate," and your aggregate participation in all "significant participation" activities exceeds five hundred hours.

5. You materially participated for any five tax years (whether or not consecutive) during the ten tax years that precede the current year.

6. Your activity is a personal service activity and you materially participated for any three tax years (whether or not consecutive) preceding the current year.

7. Based on all of the facts and circumstances, you participate on a regular, continuous, and substantial basis.

If you meet the "material participation" test in one or more activities, you'll qualify as a "real estate professional," if you meet two further tests:

1. You spend at least 750 hours per year in "real property trades or businesses" in which you materially participate. Qualifying trades or businesses include property development, redevelopment, construction, reconstruction, acquisition, conversion, rental, operation, management, leasing, and brokerage trade or business. Services you perform as an employee are *not* treated as performed in real property trades or businesses *unless* you own 5% or more of the employer entity.

2. You spend more than half of your working time on real estate activities in which you materially participate.

CHAPTER 12

MISTAKE #12:
NOT MAXIMIZING YOUR PERSONAL WEALTH WHEN CASHING OUT

"What is the difference between a taxidermist and a tax collector? The taxidermist takes only your skin."

MARK TWAIN

FOR many business owners, including myself, a lot of their net worth is tied up in their business. Doesn't it seem logical that every one of us would have a succession plan for when we retired or if we died? The truth is, most small business owners do not have a succession plan. I have helped numerous business owners with their succession planning. I often ask business owners if they have a succession plan. On many occasions I get this same response: "I am never going to retire." I will then tell them, "So immortality is your succession plan?"

This is a sticky subject for many business owners. I understand that we spend our lives growing our business, and it is hard to come to terms that someday we will no longer work in the business. I like to tell my clients, "You can have a plan by default or by design; the choice is yours."

In order to get the greatest value when you do cash out, you must plan while you are alive. Taxes can be a big part of your price, so minimizing your tax bite is essential.

Before worrying about taxes, you need a succession plan that helps you plan for the future of your business, including what happens if you should retire or pass away and maximizes what you and your family will get. It also helps to ensure that your clients are being serviced. A good succession plan starts by:

Developing a Strategy

This is the first step toward making an acquisition or seeking to sell your business. Both buyer and seller need to have a clear understanding of the goals they are seeking to achieve and how those goals will be advanced by the purchase/sale. Without a clear understanding of why a buyer or seller is involved in the deal, the less likely a deal can be executed.

Factors for consideration by a seller:

- Will I continue to work after the deal is completed?
- Who do I want to sell to?
- Will I act as a consultant to the business once the deal is completed?
- Do I want to work for a certain number of years with the buyer before the buy/sell is completed?
- Are my staff and business processes strong enough to succeed without me?
- Do I want the buyer to keep my employees?

Factors for consideration by a buyer:

- What kind of business do I want to buy?
- Do I want the owner to remain after the deal?
- Should I keep their staff?
- Do I need to increase my staff to service the new business?
- Should I buy the equipment as part of the deal?
- Should I combine the offices?

Valuation

What is the value of a business or a potential business to purchase? Getting the right valuation is a matter of personal opinion. They include;

- Net present value of future expected cash flows

- Earnings before interest, taxes, and depreciation (EBITD) multiples
- Earnings multiples
- Revenue multiples
- Asset or stock value

Identifying Buyers/Sellers

Who are you targeting to buy or sell your business to? Possible buyers/sellers include your spouse, children, partners, employees, and external third parties.

One needs to consider if the buyer/seller has the same values and type of business model that can support the deal. What kind of personality do they have? Are they rainmakers?

Evaluation and Structure of the Deal

After both the buyer and seller have identified each as a prospective match for their respective strategies, they must mutually agree on how the deal will be structured, the price, and the terms of the deal. There are a number of ways to structure the terms of the deal:

- 100% cash at closing
- Earn out by buyer or seller
- External financing

An equally important consideration is what happens post-closing and what are the expectations of each party? Should the seller remain to assist with transition? Will a different business model be implemented?

Due Diligence

Proper due diligence should be performed by both parties.

Once you do decide to sell your business, it is essential that you have a tax plan to minimize your tax expense to enhance your wealth. Here are some things to consider:

- If you're incorporated, you can sell stock. But this is rarely the best choice for smaller corporations. Buyers can't depreciate stock; they assume liability for corporate claims, and they face double tax selling appreciated assets out of C corporations.

- Your business name, client list, and goodwill are capital assets. Buyers generally depreciate these over fifteen years.

- Covenants not to compete are taxable as ordinary income to sellers, which suggests you should allocate as little of the price as possible to such agreements.

- Capital equipment such as cars, trucks, and computers is taxed as a business property. Your buyer's basis is the sale price of the asset, which he can then depreciate or expense. You'll report recaptured depreciation and capital gain.

- Inventory, supplies, and similar items that you've already expensed are taxed as ordinary income at the time of the sale.

- Continuing service after the sale is treated as earned income. Since taxes on capital gains are so much lower than taxes on earned income, it makes sense to allocate as little as possible to continued assistance after the sale.

- Real estate is taxed like any other investment property. You'll pay tax on "unrecaptured section 1250 gain" and capital gains; your buyer will depreciate it like any other property.

- If you're financing your buyer and selling depreciated assets, it may make sense to cut the amount you allocate to assets and charge more interest. This cuts tax on recaptured depreciation and may let your buyer deduct payments faster than depreciating the assets would allow.

- If you're selling one corporation to another, consider swapping your stock for your buyer's in a "qualifying reorganization" to defer tax on your gain and carry your basis in the old stock to the new.

- If your personal service is integral to your corporation's success, consider breaking out goodwill, treating it as a personal asset, and selling it separately to avoid corporate tax on that portion.

Some of these strategies could even make the sale more affordable for the buyer.

CHAPTER 13

MISTAKE #13:
MISSING TAX-COACHING SERVICES

"Did you ever notice that when you put the words 'The' and 'IRS' together, it spells 'THEIRS'?"

AUTHOR UNKNOWN

NOW that you see how business owners miss out on tax breaks, let's talk about the biggest mistake of all.

What mistake is that?

The biggest mistake of all is failing to plan. You have all heard the saying "If you fail to plan, you plan to fail." It's a cliché because it's true. Fortunately, tax-coaching service avoids the problem. A proactive tax is a written tax plan that addresses your family, home, job or business, and your investments.

There is a lot of CPA technical "stuff" in this book, but if there is one thing you should learn from this book, it's that you need the help of a qualified proactive tax coach who can legally help you pay the least amount of taxes possible. I often come across businesses whose first question to me is how much I charge for my services of tax preparation. I usually reply, "Is that the only thing you are considering?" The point here is that you should be looking for the value that the accountant brings. For example, I recently had a couple that had their tax returns done for about $800 per year. They came to me for a second opinion, and we had a mini tax-planning session where I would look for missed deductions and loopholes. I brought two ideas, which saved them about $15,000 in tax savings *per year.* I charged them a onetime tax-planning fee of $2,500 for this tax plan. Was this a good deal for the clients? What was it really costing my clients to stay with their previous accountant who was "cheap"? Had they only considered cost and not value, they would be out $15,000 per year.

So how do you know if your accountant is a good one? **It doesn't matter how good your accountant is with a stack of receipts on April 15.** It is about more than numbers. Take the following survey, and together we'll determine how valuable tax-planning service might be!

Statement 1 = Agree 5 = Strongly Disagree	5	4	3	2	1
I have a "rock-solid" tax plan that takes advantage of every opportunity the law allows.					
My current tax professional regularly brings me ideas for saving tax.					
Business					
I understand why my business is organized the way it is (e.g., proprietorship, partnership, S corporation).					
My business structure complements my future exit strategy (e.g., sale, transfer to my partners, transfer to my children).					

Benefits					
I have thoroughly evaluated my business's benefit plans and how they work together.					
My retirement plan meets my needs for current tax breaks *and* long-term investment growth.					
I have a plan to navigate the "Obamacare" rules.					
My employees understand the value of their benefits.					
Investments					
I understand how each of my investments is taxed and how it contributes to my overall portfolio tax burden.					
I have carefully considered which investments belong in taxable accounts and which investments belong in tax-advantaged accounts.					

I have a plan for maximizing the value of any long-term capital loss carry-forwards.					
I understand the rules governing "passive" income and losses and have a plan to avoid "suspended" losses.					
Charitable					
I understand how to maximize the value of my cash *and* noncash charitable contributions.					

How did you do? If the majority of your answers were disagree or strongly disagree, then it is time you get informed. You should be completely confident that you are paying the least amount in taxes; if you are not, you should get a second opinion. Remember the old tax saying, "It's not what you earn, it's what you keep."

In addition, ask yourself these questions:

- Do you see your accountant only when you drop off your documents?
- Can you even get a hold of your accountant between February and April 15?
- When was the last time your accountant gave you an idea to save you money?

- Do you have a tax-planning meeting before year's end?
- How do they keep up with all the rules and regulations?
- How much business experience do they have?
- What designations do they hold?

Remember, it is not what you earn...It is what you keep!

CHAPTER 14

RIDICULOUS TAX
DEDUCTIONS

THERE is a difference between legal tax deductions and being aggressive. Some people get outright creative when coming up with their tax deductions. The Minnesota Society of Certified Public Accountants (MNCPA) recently surveyed its CPA members about the most creative tax deductions proposed by their clients. Here are some of the most memorable responses from the 2012 MNCPA annual list of strange and unacceptable tax deductions.

- A ballerina was shocked to discover that she couldn't deduct the cost of a tummy tuck. Maybe she should just go on a diet?

- One woman attempted to deduct Botox expenses as an "image enhancement" expense. You know the old saying, "Looks aren't everything."

- Don't try to claim your manicures as a business expense, as one piano player proposed. How about claiming your piano lessons instead?

- A farmer who tried to claim food and veterinary expenses for his toy poodle as a farm building "guard dog." Doesn't the IRS know that a dog is a man's best friend?

- One woman took a chance on deducting gambling losses as a charity donation. I guess she was bad at gambling, because she could have offset any losses with winnings. Maybe she would be better off just donating money to charity instead of gambling; at least it goes to a good cause.

- Although children/dependents are considered an acceptable deduction, one filer failed to realize that he needed to actually have children/dependents in order to claim them. Oh, those little bundles of joy, which I refer to at tax time as my little tax deductions.

- One person tried to deduct tanning-bed expenses. As if burning your skin wasn't bad enough for you.

- One woman hoped to shed some pounds and add a deduction by writing off the cost of Zumba exercise classes. "¡Ay, caramba!"

As you can see, people do get creative. The point here is that you will always need to defend a deduction to the IRS. If you have any doubt that you can't defend it, *then don't do it!*

William G. (Bill) Cummings, CPA, CTC, and PFS, serves as President of Cummings Financial Organization. He has been in the financial services business for the past twenty-five years, helping his clients make sound financial decisions, including how to pay the least amount in taxes, retirement planning, investment planning, insurance planning, estate planning, elder care planning, and insurance planning. Bill acts as a "chief financial officer" for his clients, both for businesses and individuals. He coordinates all aspects of their financial matters to help his clients spend more time on things they love to do.

Bill also served as the controller and chief financial officer of a large financial services firm.

Bill and his wife, Kimberli, reside in beautiful Tampa, Florida; they have five children. He and his wife are active in their community. They support various charities in the Tampa Bay community.